COME VIBE WITH ME...

Pocket Love Poetry

Dre Pierre

Published by The Moving Pen, 2022.

POCKET LOVE POETRY

First edition. September 13, 2022.

ISBN: 979-8986573434

Written by Dre Pierre.

Table of Contents

This book is dedicated to my father who is truly missed and is unable to be here to witness.

And to my Mother who is nothing but supportive of my journey in writing.

CHAPTER 1

the journey

Pocket Love Poetry is the gift and the curse. This is the story of love and its journey...

4/19 was the best day of my life. We had 50 of our closest friends and family standing over the sands of Miami beach as we spread our vow of love. This poem also sums up our bond and the strong foundation that crumbled like a cookie in a child's hand. It was a marriage that lasted five years, and now the journey begins all over again. Where is the love?

4/19

There was a moment within your eyes that said "yes",

and everything moved harmonically,

playing in sync with a flute and soft vocals.

There wasn't a kiss, but our words mingled like soft porn.

It was nothing too expletive, but our vibes rolled with our lives.

A COOKIE

I have shredded tears amongst the stars

and submerged my head in the deep blue.

My addiction to my happiness seems to be covered

like naked people on public access TV.

I can't fight my way through every battle

because the years have worn on my soul.

I am hitting a pivotal point!

My energy has been depleted to under 50 percent.

This video game of life is pushing my boundaries,

squeezing my heart,

and ripping

the fabric of happiness from my mind.

Yet I must still find that golden light

So it can guide me to a level of good.

But like fairytales, stories are only written to uplift.

The outside world is much more like

a roller-coaster ride without any restraints.

I step through muddy waters with patten leather shoes,

thinking the stains can be removed

but instead, I leave my only regret behind

progress.

Time does not rewind

and the past is a roadmap of where you have been.

This is the perfect study for my journey,

and all I want is a cookie

the way my two-year-old wants one,

A cookie to make everything okay.

Temporary is better than never,

so I will indulge in a cookie

a chocolate chip deluxe

like pain pills for an addict

hoping I overdose on happiness.

Five years, and we are done. There's nothing left but my demise, and I must regather my mind to seek out what I thought I might have been missing. There is no time to rewind. All I have is a forward-moving action to grow and nurture what I lost.

PUSHING FORWARD

There's a mystical thought

submerged within my conscience.

I'm overlayed by lonely ideas,

so, I come to conclude

my vast vocabulary of wall-talk graffiti

in simple layman's terms:

I want what I want,

and emotions cannot dictate my forward push,

or else I will become another statistic

of cupid's reckless arrow tossing.

Not every landing place can be a home.

Even maggots begin at a side-carcass left after its loss.

And I'm no dinner, but I am an unopened jar

filled with the abundance of

Life, Love, and Happiness.

We must share the same graphic painting

or risk the handle of my grip slip

because I no longer roll.

Instead, I move like poetry in the raw

That's sought out like a whirlwind

swirling through suburbs and hoods,

bringing all along for the ride,

but only one will push forward

through my chaotic portrait

and see the Mona Lisa smile and know

We are home.

I realize life moves with or without you, and I must start to venture into the world of dating. Two failed marriages have me a little reluctant to give my all or show my all. I'm still tender from all these turbulent thoughts.

My Bloody Tears

There's something within my memory

that regurgitates my deepest fears,

but my fast-moving heart paces

beyond the rim of meditated thoughts.

I am anemic by my very movement.

All can be one and one is with all.

There is nothing within my words

that can pull me from the sunken place

because I have already fixed my posture

for any failed attempts to love.

It's something my body craves and my soul desires,

but my outer layer fades away any reddish hue

only because my heart is afraid to fall

like the 10,000-mile plunge from jumping out of a plane.

Except when this heart travels,

there's hope that a parachute would appear

because I have hit the ground a thousand times

with nothing but hope guiding my life.

Like the sand blows away from a light gust of wind,

my bloody tears have removed all the pain I have harbored.

I started that slow process called dating and put myself out there as a rare mess who's not ready to seek but hoping to find. The combination of lust and love is a mixture that should not be taken for granted.

Movement

My mind is heavy with thoughts of the past

as I nudge my way through the gritty angles of hope.

I've become numb to the idea love is a foundation of deep thoughts that formulate an outstanding partner. But something inside can't help my emotions.

Unstable Emotions

I was drenched in vocabulary muck

because I uttered the sacred three words

every man's soul yearns

to be covered in like Mom's milk.

We only want what any human creature seeks:

that hand-knotted bond,

even though we must display the armor of Thor.

Nothing could penetrate my grill

until I saw you smile.

It was more than the key for a lock;

It was a combination for my coded tongue.

We connected without any physical contact,

and when we nudged the notion,

I stumbled my way to a forbidden fruit

that left me aghast by your internal allure.

The scene wasn't painted as a portrait of romance,

but the chemistry of our bodies transposed the norm.

Our daily growth has

watered my soul and sparked my heart,

leaving me disorientated to

what I feel, when I feel, how I feel

It's an emotional roller-coaster ride

as I continue to whirl around

until the seat next to me is filled

with a thrill-seeking spirit

that I'm anticipating is you.

The quest for a partner is a long journey of trial and error. There's an illusion that what we find is a treasury in the bodies we meet, but the reality is that we find a show in front of the curtain. Everything is revealed after the show has ended.

VOIDED ILLUSIONS

I never thought I would be at a loss for words.

Empty inside a library, they have smeared into dust.

There is no filter in my life.

I just replay the reruns like an old man in his recliner.

On one hand, my dreams swirl in icy brown liquid.

On the other hand, life burns slowly with a stench.

I may have desecrated my dreams

with the silly notion of love

by trying to fulfill that fortified structure of commitment.

Everything I received is a lesson learned as a side note,

and I can only wonder:

Am I doomed because I did not read the fine print

and handle with care or will Karma appear?

There are basic rules in dating, and we tend to miss out on the most important ones. A red flag is a red flag and even a blind man senses change.

EXPOSED

I exposed too much of myself

to the rays of the sun.

I am not butter or ice.

but I have melted my emotions

across the table of trust.

The acknowledgment remained silent.

Chapter 2

rummage

DISBURSE ENERGY

There is an indication within my stare

that drifts beyond kinetic thoughts

and I am flustered by my energy

because it loops without any connection

like a static shock ten times the volt,

leaving me babbling like a baby

because my structure has collapsed

before the foundation could harden.

Where do I stand?

When my energy sparks the flames; without air,

nothing can breathe life.

The Holding Cell

I'm drifting to a place

where my mind can soak the sins of my past.

The angels have been awakened by my awareness,

and I have failed to seek refuge.

Now I'm walking through the desert,

feeling the lonely heat

and breathing in the dead air.

My eyes are open,

and my lungs fill with the taste of defeat.

I'm near my final days, looking for a rope

hoping to rekindle the spark

that held my innocent soul together

when sin wasn't a part of my accessories.

I am drifting,

and I know I will soon follow the path of the fallen,

where knowledge will be bestowed upon me

and peppered across old flames.

and I will then ask myself if I can endure the lit candle

because my painted stones have faded

with my watery reflection.

This is when everything seems to go downhill. The divorce seems to be the snowball effect of the avalanche of love that is bestowed upon my feet. I'm lost within words spewing from my soul, only to render the thoughts of lost hope.

My Whispered Words

I whisper words onto your tongue

and slowly caress the air from your lungs.

Without a syllable leaving my throat,

my fingerprints would be a clue.

I have nothing within the bare essence of the notion

because the holding cell is my home.

And I use my teeth like guarded jails,

protecting what so many throw away.

Like a little kid, I hide behind my silly laugh.

I'm lost like the rabbit

stumbling over my generic thoughts.

I'm not sure if those three words

can be a fixture in my abode.

I know the color of foliage

as it falls through light air,

but I am unsure of the dense

posture you bestow in my presence.

I'm twisted in every direction,

feeling like a trespasser in a garden of roses.

Thorns rip from core

because you can no longer protect

what has already been wounded.

The aura that is your light

holds you together like a soldier at war,

but even water can overtake

any emotional waves hiding in the dark.

Tattoo waves

I'm dried up with emotional outbreaks

and low-vision thoughts.

I portrayed the future of my existence

in the hands of unrested souls.

This world has too many lurking ideas

and not enough words backed by actions,

leaving me to pour the foundation of old soul talk

left from previous generations.

We can be as simplified as a dog in a cage,

except our cage is open

and we have been trained to sit.

So, I've looked for my journey to be within

crowded rooms and tobacco smoke sections,

hoping I can play out any last-minute celebration

with a enmesh point of laughter

because nothing is as authentic

as a kiss under the moon.

We all have hidden agendas

and unopen thoughts

about life's mysterious goals.

I have only one question to ponder

as I lie there baffled to my core:

Where could there be love

if our hands are soiled with filth?

Then, somewhere out of the darkness, came the connection of unspoken words where we vibe like no other.

THE GRIP

There is a fraction of my soul

under the sign of construction,

and I'm uneven with my light footwork.

I have a simple complicated idea

that we can forge more-than-unwilling emotions

and connect where our bodies inside impulse

pulsate more from passionate deliberation.

But where is our flow?

Where my skin integrates with your glow

and you gently moan when I pull your soul

closer to mine.

I'm looking deep into your eyes,

and that's not me gazing for touch

because I have already entered the forbidden land

and submerged my all within your walls,

sending an electric shock as we melt in the winter heat

and sweating as we swell to an erupting roar.

Like the waves of the ocean

after a hurricane has passed.

we lay calm to the substance.

We have bonded the physical with the spiritual;

the mental with the emotional,

The only question to arise from our minds is:

"Where do our roads go?"

Pure Bliss

The moment of pure bliss

is a timeless entry

when looking at your earthly tones.

A man can't stay away from water,

even if he is drowning

An addiction, you are not.

You are more like that vital organ

a body needs to survive,

and I'm counting to ten

because my mind has lost conscience.

Your exquisiteness has poured into my veins.

My vision is cloudy, some will say,

but I know where I roam.

And with a snap of the finger, you were gone. I thought I found love, but it was diluted by social desires. My lonely heart steps out again, but this time, I add a layer of armor.

I realize I'm compatible with everyone, but not everyone is compatible with me.

Energy

Take it upon your soul

to intermingle with my mood.

Understand my majestic melodies;

They're like waves on a full moon.

A Thought

When I rose in the morning,

I was burdened by my overnight thoughts.

I had no dreams or nightmares,

but somehow, you were there

like a mist with the early morning breeze,

and I inhaled the essence of your ambiance

only to be left wondering:

Are my eyes wide shut?

I'm holding air as if the molecular

vibed off my vibration.

And just like that, through the dating game app, you appeared. You were always there, but this time, we talked and there was a spark.

I'm Focused on You

There are a thousand pictures

painted within my mind,

and I'm focused on you,

I heard a thousand stories

about how I can be loved,

but I'm focused on you.

A man doesn't see a rainbow looking for gold

when all along, his soul has blackened the earth.

There's more to the unwritten path of Love,

and the idea that the word **everlasting**, is real

can leave me to the center of my emotions

and have me filter through my past regressions

to overcome any outstanding lust

and understand that the faithful have arrived.

I'm left bewildered by my closed-off mind

that you ripped off like a beer top.

You are the one like the cliché in a movie.

But in real-life action, we blend without physical touch.

And I have lost a dozen words

trying to describe our ventures,

but I know the boundaries of our touch

will reshape our awkward flow

and lead us to a journey

many wish they could have

but only few have walked the path,

where friends and love will interlock our behavior

to a place where we talk in silence and make love

like Beethoven's music notes.

It started with simple text messages that blossomed like a carnation white flower in a pot. Now we are bonding and connecting, but there is that thorn that accompanies any beautiful rose. Your thorn is an attachment. You are attached to the highest level of commitment, and I'm standing in the shadows wondering why won't I leave...

Heavy Addiction

My mind is a heavy addiction

that's filled with constant images and words

of where we intertwined with our thoughts.

I have overdosed so much

on the air you exhale

that I suffocated my idea

of what a commitment can truly become.

I know that if I remain silent,

the waves of my affection

will crash upon the shores of an island

that is lost beyond the deep blue sea.

So, without the pen or pad, I will stand and firmly say:

We need to upgrade our vocabulary from a verb to a noun

so our sentences can blossom into a story

written from our soul

and guided by the divine.

So I take one step forward,

idling for you to stand on my side.

There's a void left in my mind, but awkward thoughts progress through distant eyes until the darkness foreshadows my intuition, now I see nothing but mortiferous love from malignant opinions.

The Storm

I'm measured by

my belligerent thoughts of past algorithms,

where I was bonded twice

and accused of slaughtering

a dozen rose petals in my path.

Moving like an unstable tornado,

I feel I'm more like a hurricane,

storming through the ideas

many have tossed my way,

and I see no authentic flow.

They can't see the calm in my eye,

but they think every word is a lie

because my language of love

is on a frequency of an emotional tone.

All I hear is what you want and what you need,

and it's me, me, me!

I'm alone to ponder where I belong,

but maybe the hunt shouldn't be achieved.

Perhaps it should be left to nature to fulfill my needs,

where I can find that one rose

that lives longer than a smile from the heart.

That's when I'll open

and reveal everything you need to know,

and that will be the calm

surrounded by the storm.

The next book:
Coffee & Words

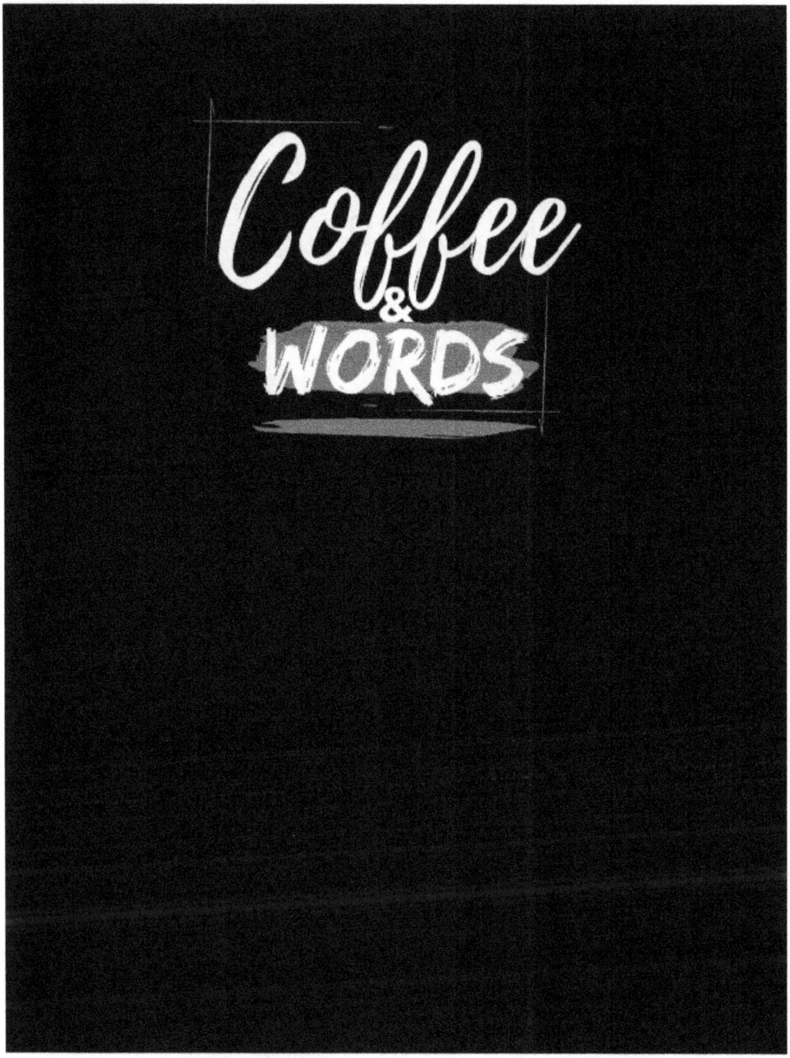
Coffee
&
WORDS

EXPERINCE THE NEXT VIBE OF POETRY IN COFFEE & WORDS

The Moving Pen

Where Ideas begin...

Don't miss out!

Visit the website below and you can sign up to receive emails whenever Dre Pierre publishes a new book. There's no charge and no obligation.

https://books2read.com/r/B-A-XZZU-NGZAC

BOOKS 2 READ

Connecting independent readers to independent writers.

About the Author

My poetry is my soul.

I was born in the borough of Queens. New York is where the sounds of a busy city whispered melodic tunes to the fingerprints of my heart. A city that can easily manifest the most creative ideas and I'm proud to be born and raised there. This is where my poetry came to life. I started writing in elementary school. Poetry gave me a way to express myself and my journey began with my first feeling of love. I write with a passion in my poetry as well as in my short stories and songs. Everything I do is with the feelings from my soul.

Read more at https://drepoet.com.